I0142358

WALKING WORTHY

I Surrender All

DIANE PACE

Walking Worthy:

I Surrender All

Diane Pace

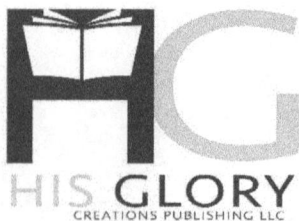

HIS GLORY

CREATIONS PUBLISHING LLC

www.hisglorycreationspublishing.com

PRAISE FOR

Walking Worthy: I Surrender All

"Once I read the chapters of this book, I began to reflect back through the years of my wife's Christian journey. I have watched my loving wife of 23 years grow spiritually. I have watched her humble herself to be obedient to those that have leadership over her. My wife, Minister Diane Pace, takes her walk with God serious. Di is a humble servant. I've listened to her pray for others even when she was going through struggles herself. My wife has been the glue that bonds our family. She is a woman of God that believes in praising her way through whatever trials come her way. My wife loves researching, studying and learning about the Word of God. She is a servant that believes in doing God's Perfect Will. I have watched her silently deal with the curveballs that life has thrown her way. I've seen her "down for the count" many times, but through God, she bounced back from life's blows. Di is genuinely very supportive of others. I see her enthusiasm as she works at our church, Delightful Temple Ministries. She also blesses others through her book ministry, Walking Worthy, works with Women of Triumph Ministries, works behind the scenes with His Glory Creations Publishing and faithfully supports Polish Your Diamond.

She strives to bless and encourage others through her book ministry. As I write this endorsement, my eyes and my heart are flowing with tears of joy. God has kept His promise that she would write books. My wife is a living testimony of a servant walking worthy. Therefore, I'm honored to endorse my wife's first solo book, Walking Worthy: I surrender All."

I love you Di.
Your Loving Husband, Raymond Pace

"My mother's book, Walking Worthy: I Surrender All, really takes me to a relatable time. My mother, Minister Diane Pace, raised her children in St. James Church under Bishop Holder too. I can remember my daddy, Raymond Pace, being baptized in that same river. Through the years, it has been a pleasure hearing her stories about her childhood in church. Now, as an adult, being able to read about times in her life is phenomenal. I'm better able to understand her walk with God. It's amazing. It is with great honor that I endorse my mother's first of many solo books, Walking Worthy: I Surrender All. I am very proud of you, Momma."

I Love You,
Your Loving Son, Dex Brown

"I am honored to endorse my baby sister's book, Walking Worthy: I Surrender All. Minister Diane Pace, we love you. You have grown a beautiful life with Christ, your husband and family. You help everybody."

Love you!
Your big sister, Brenda Turner

"I have watched your struggles, and I've watched you grow into the woman of God that you are. I'm glad to see how God is blessing you."

Your Loving Mother,
Frances Turner

"I am honored and pleased to endorse my Mother in-law, Minister Diane Pace, as an author and a woman of God. Through the years I have known her, she has been a loving and honest mother figure for me. Her pursuit of God, righteousness, and enlightenment are an inspiration to all. Her ministry as an author will be a blessing to all who partake in the spiritual food offered. Again, I am honored and overjoyed to offer my endorsement of an amazing woman of God."

Your Son in Love,
Derek Walker

"It is with great pleasure that I endorse my mother, Minister Diane Pace, as an author. This amazing woman of God is on fire for the Lord and eager to grow spiritually. Many relationships in our church, community and family, have been strengthened and enriched through the use of Minister Diane allowing God to use her to be a blessing to so many people. Her book is well written, engaging and biblically based, with numerous insights from Minister Diane's years of spiritual upbringing, growth and experiences. I am ecstatic to endorse her as a woman of God and author of Walking Worthy: I Surrender All."

"Train up a child in the way he should go; and when he is old, he will not depart from it." -Proverbs 22:6

Your Loving Baby Girl,
Renee Walker

"Diane is such a phenomenal woman of God in whom I admire for her faithfulness to the body of Christ as a whole. Her passion for God's work is above and beyond...."Eye hath not seen, nor ear heard, neither have entered into the heart of man, the things which God has prepared for those who love Him" (1 Corinthians 2:9).

Pastor Corey Williams-Brown,
Mincey Chapel Church, Kenly, North Carolina

"In appreciation of Minister Pace's contribution to the body of Christ, I feel privileged to write this notation of her outstanding character and service. She is destined for greatness. Minister Pace has been a blessing to our church family and serves tirelessly in her outreach ministry. She is very tenacious and steadfast. Once she has a goal in mind, she is determined to follow through. She is a student of the bible and seeks to attend classes to enhance her knowledge and continuing education.

I am excited that her profound message of "Walking Worthy" is circulating around the community and the various churches. Her message of encouragement and testimonies will continue to bless many people. It is a pleasure to serve with her in ministry."

Pastor Carolynn Robinson
Delightful Temple Ministries, Kenly, North Carolina

"We count it a privilege to endorse Minister Diane Pace. Diane has been in ministry for over four years. She currently serves as Membership Coordinator and Public Relations and Marketing Assistant. She has given faithful service. As an author, she will be an asset to His Glory Creations Publishing. She is well respected by those who know her, even by those of other religion persuasion. I believe that Minister Diane has encouraged others like me to become an author. She will publish more books, motivate, and uplift others to follow their dream. Minister Diane's honor and confidentiality will always be a bonus for her. She strives to become a best-selling author in her projects. Without reservation and with full endorsement on the behalf of the CEO-Director and on behalf of the Executive Board, we commend you."

Pastor Anna J Lyons
CEO-Director Women of Triumph Ministry

"It is with great joy that I endorse Minister Diane Pace as an author. This young lady has been in the gospel ministry for over four years. She totally understands her calling and is determined, with God›s blessing, to undertake this great work as a published author.

She will do all she can to meet the criteria for this endeavor. Dianne has been a true example with her family, church, and community to follow your dreams. I have witnessed firsthand her work ethics and her love, and compassion for lost souls. I am pleased to endorse her as a true Woman of God and Author of Walking Worthy: I Surrender All."

Yours in Christ, Apostle Robert Johnson
Senior Pastor of Pentecostal Temple COGIC,
2722 Wabash Street, Michigan City, Indiana 46360

"Walking Worthy is a true testimony of Minister Diane Pace's commitment to live a holy, separated life for Christ. Her transparency is proof that the freedom in living for Christ, which can only come from God above, allows His children to minister healing and deliverance to those who desire to know Him in the fullness of His glory. Reading this book is a definite must for people of all walks of life, who want to draw closer to the Lord, and overcome Satan's plot to keep mankind from experiencing God's grace in its fullness."

Elder Joel Emerson M. Walker and Evangelist Julia Walker Pastor
and First Lady of New Vision Ministries Church of God in Christ, Alcoa, Tennessee

"Minister Dianne Pace is a best-selling author of the anthologies: Down for The Count Bouncing Back from Life's Blows Volumes l and ll. Her first solo book, Walking Worthy: I Surrender All, is a personal story of triumph over trials and tribulations to walk worthy of her calling in God. Great read and insightful look into what it means to walk worthy."

Author Elder Pamela Horne,
contributing author of Down for the Count: Bouncing Back from Life's Blows Volume II and III. CEO of Consuming Fire Book Ministries

"I would just like to commend you for telling and sharing with us your story. A lot of us are still in problems like that today but choose to try to hide the truth. You have inspired me to have a closer relationship with God as well. To see you and Raymond began to walk together as one has given me a better look on... can saved women draw an unsaved man to Christ? Yes, you have lived according to God's way and now I see growth in your husband. So proud of you Minister Diane Pace and your book ministry Walking Worthy. Keep your eyes on God and let him continue to lead and guide you on this journey. Love you, and it is always a pleasure to work with you."

Humbly, Your cousin, Bishop Renea Harris
SOW TWO GOD MINISTRY

"I'm so proud of you, Grandma Diane. All of my life, you have made sure Mommy took me to church. I really appreciate you. I love the chapters you wrote in Down for The Count: Bouncing Back from Life's blows. I know Walking Worthy: I Surrender All is going to help someone learn about God."

I love you so much,
DiZarria Brown

"I am proud and glad to endorse Minister Diane Pace. Diane is truly an example of a Woman of God and a servant for Kingdom building. It›s rare that you can meet someone which whom you instantly connect, especially divine connections. Diane is truly someone who is a giver as well as a lover. Diane and I Co-Authored in Down for The Count Volume 2 and her chapter touched my heart. Diane truly is an author at heart. You can feel her words as if you were there. One of the scriptures that best fit Diane is...Do nothing from selfishness or empty conceit, but with humility of mind regard one another as more important than yourselves; do not merely look out for your own personal interests but also for the interests of others. Have this attitude in yourselves which was also in Christ Jesus. – Philippians 2:3-5. When I say God has his hands on Diane, I genuinely and truly mean that. The fruit she is bearing and pouring into others is awesome."

God Bless You,
Louvanta White-Horne

"I dedicate my blessings and prayers to my sister in Christ, Minister Diane. She and I have grown up together since kindergarten, so I definitely remember the days of old. Chapter One brought back many memories. I thank God for seeing how she has grown spiritually. God is opening doors for Minister Diane to use the book ministry, Walking Worthy, to reach people all over. Through the years, God has elevated her, and she is a blessing to many. What a small "fireball" she has turned out to be on this Christian journey. Minister Diane, continue to throw your net out for even greater things, in Jesus' name. My sister is truly walking worthy of her calling. It is a privilege and honor to endorse her first solo book, Walking Worthy: I Surrender All."

Love you Sis,
Elder Towanda Battle

"We love Minister Diane. She is a remarkable woman of God. She has supported Pastor Burnie and me in all of our ministry events. She has joined me on empowerment calls as well as speaking during our seminars. She was also a vendor at my Polish Your Diamond seminars. She is a great encouragement and is always ready to support and help out in any way that she can. Everyone needs a Minister Diane in their lives. I am sure that God will continue to push her forward into greater for all the sacrifices she has made for others. We love you, Minister Diane. You are worthy of the crown."

Pastor Burnice Burroughs and Co-Pastor Teresia Miller Burroughs
Life Coaches and Authors of Polish Your Diamond and Relatable Relationships
Pastor and Co-Pastor at Holy Transformation Empowerment, Center Raleigh NC

"It is truly a pleasure and an honor to endorse the book, Walking Worthy. Minister Diane Pace is a walking testimony and an inspiration for women and the community. I love the chapters that I have had the pleasure to read and I'm looking forward to reading the rest of the book."

Jeremy Wheless
Vice President- Richard Harris Funeral Home & Cremation Service

"My mother, Diane Pace is an important part of my life. She gives me positive lead way to keep me on the right track with my Lord and Savior. I'm her oldest son, Jeffrey Pace, and with the love I have for her, I would like to endorse my lovely mother, Minister Diane Pace, as an author. I've watched the amazing things God has brought her through. Minister Diane Pace is a strong, powerful woman of God. I've seen

God bless this wonderful woman with spiritual growth and experiences. It's a blessing to see Minister Diane Pace as the author of Walking Worthy: I Surrender All."

Colossians 1:10-11, "That ye might walk worthy of the Lord unto all pleasing, being fruitful in every good work, and increasing in the knowledge of God; Strengthened with all might, according to his glorious power, unto all patience and longsuffering with joyfulness."

I Love You, Mom,
Your oldest son, Jeffrey Pace

"I'm honored to endorse my mother's first solo book, Walking Worthy: I surrender All. I'm so proud of my mother and the many blessings she's receiving. My mother, Minister Diane Pace, has worked so hard to get where she is today. She faithfully raised us in church. Every Sunday, we knew there were no excuses. Even when I would lose a sock, Mom would say, 'You're going to church anyway with or without that sock.' I have watched her survive life's obstacles and situations. Those trials only made her a stronger person. My mom's book ministry has inspired me to live a better life. I watch my mom walk worthy in her calling. I would not change her for anything. Thanks mom. Congratulations! I'm so proud of you."

Love You Much,
Your Baby Son, Lil Raymond

"Sis, I've watched you grow through the tender years and mature into the golden years. I'm elated to have traveled part of the journey with you. I've always admired your relentless drive to conquer the events of life. I've witnessed your bold perseverance to strive for abundance. You have allowed God to use you for His glory. I'm very proud of you and your accomplishments. It is with great pleasure that I endorse your book, Walking Worthy: I Surrender All."

Love you dearly sis, Trena Hines
Author and CEO of Love Unlimited Book Ministry

"Minister Diane Pace started out at St James church in Middlesex NC under the leadership of the late Rev. Sylvester Holder. This is where she got rooted in Christ. Diane's mother, Frances Turner, and I raised our children in St. James church together. Growing up Minister Diane often thought that we saints didn't know how to go home. As a woman of God, Minister Diane always stayed ready to do God's work. She always responded with a "yes" when called upon. She always followed through with her response. I salute her on her walk with Christ. I salute her book, Walking Worthy: I Surrender All. May God bless her always."

James 2:26, "For as the body without the spirit is dead, so faith without works is dead also."

Love you,
Aunt Mary Lou Hinton

"What a pleasure to know this young lady. I have known this woman of God practically all of my life. Minister Diane Pace is truly a great woman of strength and integrity. She is full of Zeal for Christ.

I'm excited for what and where God is taking her. Based on what I know and have read so far, I was blessed. I know that readers will be enriched and empowered even more. Minister Diane and I serve together in Women of Triumph Ministries. I have read both of the Down for The Count: Bouncing Back from Life's Blows Anthologies Volume I and II. I was blessed by her testimonies. I am honored to endorse her book, Walking Worthy: I Surrender All. I pray that it blesses all that read it."

Love you Sis,
Unetta Lofton

Minister Diane Pace wrote a very inspiring and moving work about her relationship with God and her upbringing in the church. Her transparency shown through this book will help so many others who have experienced very similar situations. I celebrate what God is doing through her in the literary world! Congratulations on releasing your first solo book!

Felicia Lucas, Publisher
His Glory Creations Publishing LLC

I feel blessed to be able to read the Journey of the author, with the two of us growing up together. I truly remember the incidents she has recalled. It is evident that children pay attention to the elders no matter what generation it may be. Our upbringing was a firm foundation for our adulthood. Knowing that God's word is true, we now can admit as children we thought we knew the answer, but in truth we did not know the answers and time will change opinions but never the truth. This is a book that I hope many will read. I am so proud of you Diane! Continue to follow Christ and let his word show in all you do.

I wish you God's speed.

Rev. Dr. S.W. Holder
Pastor St. James Church of Christ.

Copyright © 2019 by Diane Pace

All rights reserved. No part of this book may be reproduced in any form without permission in writing from the publisher, except in the case of brief quotations embodied in critical articles or reviews. Unauthorized reproduction of any part of this work is illegal and is punishable by law.

The author and publisher shall have neither liability nor responsibility for anyone with respect to any loss or damage caused directly or indirectly, by the information contained in this book.

ISBN: 978-1-950861-04-0

Scripture references are used with permission from Zondervan via Biblegateway.com

Printed in the United States of America

10 9 8 7 6 5 4 3 2 1

CONTENTS

This book is dedicated to anyone struggling to live righteous. It is intended to help anyone that does not understand the power of forgiveness. Walking Worthy is a heartfelt book written to help someone that may have backslid or has forgotten your first love... God. Perhaps you're struggling with church hurt. Be encouraged and know that the joy of the Lord is your strength. I pray that this book blesses everyone that reads it.

Acknowledgements

I WOULD LIKE TO express my gratitude to the many people who saw me through this book; Thank You, God. Thanks to my mother, Frances Turner, for my godly upbringing. Thanks to my pastor, Carolynn Robinson and her husband Deacon Moses Robinson, for always encouraging me. Thanks to Pastor Anna Lyons and the Women of Triumph Ministries for your support. Thank you to Apostle Robert Johnson for the many prophetic words. I'm grateful to my daughter, Renee Walker and my sister Brenda Turner, for encouraging me every step of the way. I'm grateful to my husband, Raymond Pace, for the love, support, always believing in me and encouraging me to share my testimony. Thank you to my publisher, Minister Felicia Lucas, for enabling me to publish my story.

INTRODUCTION

A RE YOU WALKING WORTHY as a child of God? This includes the challenge to stop complaining. As I walk this journey of Christian life, I often find myself doing a self-examination. When I gave my life to Christ, I had to make a change. In order to walk worthy as a child of God, I needed to be spiritually cleansed. It wasn't enough to just get saved. I needed to be converted. I sometimes ask myself, "Are you sure that was Christ-like? Have you sold out to God?" I constantly evaluate my relationship with God.

In this book, I share my story of my walk with God. I tell of my experiences in church from childhood till current day. Some of my experiences were comical and some were dark moments. To stay on the straight and narrow path, I had to put on the whole armor of God. In order to walk worthy, I had to surrender all to God. I wanted to share my story to give others hope. As you read my book, it is my hope that it will inspire you to live a righteous life. I pray that every reader is inclined to have a closer walk with God.

"That ye might walk worthy of the Lord unto all pleasing, being fruitful in every good work, and increasing in the knowledge of God."

Colossians 1:10

CHAPTER ONE

....

Growing Up in Church

GOD HAS ALWAYS BEEN a large part of my life. As a single parent, my mother raised seven children in church. Our home church was St. James in Middlesex, N. C. The late Bishop, Sylvester Holder was the pastor. St. James is where my Christian foundation was established. Bishop Holder and his wife, the late Ruby Holder, along with my mother Frances Turner, my cousin Mary Lou Hinton and a few others started St. James Church. Thanks to my first Sunday school teacher, the late Wilma Jean Holder Lewis, St. James is where I first learned to love unconditionally. Although I was very young, I learned a lot about Christianity and about the love of God. Jean planted a seed of love in me at a very early age.

Being able to love the way God intended us to love is a part of walking worthy. Our Christian faith was holiness; therefore, we lived by certain guidelines. I would frequently see the movement of God in our church through so many actions. There was always praising, worshiping, prophesying, shouting, acts of kindness, support of others, casting out demons, communion, washing feet, deliverance and healings. I grew up witnessing saints walking worthy. I can remember Bishop Holder wanting transportation to get his members to church, so they made a way to get a church bus. St. James had a big green church bus that Bishop used to transport the members to and from church services. Kids that didn't go to church had labeled St. James kids the "Holy Ghost kids". During this time, I was between 4 and 10 years old. I hated going to church. One day, we were all at the river for someone's baptism. I can remember the members standing on the riverbank singing, 'Take Me to The Water'. As the members were singing, I blurted out, "We're already at the damn water!" As a child, it seemed holy people did not know how to go home.

It seemed like they were always tarrying at the altar. Although I hated going, I would always be drawn in, either by the sermon or the altar call. There was always something about those parts of the service that stirred my spirit. There was something about the Word that was preached that caused people to get saved and some delivered. I used to think, "Wow, Bishop Holder really knows God. Look at these people getting saved." Little did I know, Bishop Holder was walking worthy and was allowing God to use him. In 1975, we moved to Zebulon, and since my mother didn't drive, we weren't able to attend church at St. James. Although we weren't able to attend, my mother continued to keep us in church. Through the years, my mother would visit St.

James when she could. Services at other churches were different and much quieter. I wasn't as interested in the services, so I was easily distracted. I can remember attending church and sitting next to my sister, Shirley. Shirley would say comical things under her breath, and I would always bust out in laughter.

One particular Sunday, one of the older ladies in church came in after service had started. Shirley whispered, "No wonder she's late. She had to go kill that fox around her neck." I slowly turned to see what she meant, and there stood a woman with some type of fur draped around her neck. I got so tickled and let out a loud laugh. There are so many fond memories of growing up in church. Although I hated going to church as a child, I thank God for my upbringing (Proverbs 22:6). Train up a child in the way he should go, and when he is old, he will not depart from it.

Unfortunately, as I got older, I strayed from my first love, God. I cursed and used the words very well. I was quick tempered and very headstrong. I was always the black sheep of the family. I was always different, outspoken, blunt and straight forward. Romans 8:30-31, "And so those whom God set apart, he called; and those he called, he put right with himself, and he shared his glory with them. In view of all this, what can we say? If God is for us, who can be against us?" Through the years, I learned to walk worthy of calling myself a child of God, saved or a Christian.

CHAPTER TWO

Life in Church as an Adult

W HEN MY YOUNGEST SON was born, I was invited to become a part of a local church. In 1991, I joined that church. During the time I was there, I was living in sin. I was "shacking" and knew it was ungodly. I had been raised in church, and I knew right from wrong. I knew I was not worthy of calling myself a child of God, saved, converted, holy nor righteous. Proverbs 3:5,6 states, "Trust in the Lord with all thine heart; and lean not unto thine own understanding. In all thy ways acknowledge him, and he shall direct thy paths."

As I kept going to church, the desire to walk worthy grew stronger. Matthew 5:6 reads, "Blessed are those who hunger and thirst for righteousness, for they shall be satisfied." As an adult Christian, I have always had a very strong desire to know as much about God and walking right in God's eyes. I take my Christian journey very serious. To me, God is real, and I want to be real. (John 4:24) reminds us, "God *is* Spirit, and those who worship Him must worship in spirit and truth." God sits high and looks low, and God have no respect of person. Romans 2:11-16 states, "For there is no respect of persons with God." I began to seek God for answers, wondering why I was so thirsty for more and more. God showed me that there was much more for me. He let me know I needed to surrender all. God is Holy, and I needed to live holy. Psalm 99 warns us, "The Lord, our God is Holy. The Lord reigns; let the peoples tremble! He sits enthroned upon the cherubim; let the earth quake! The Lord is great in Zion; he is exalted over all the peoples. Let them praise your great and awesome name! Holy is he!

One day, my siblings asked if I would visit St. James. Since none of us had been back there in years, I agreed. Once at St. James, I felt what I had been longing for. I was in an environment of spirit and truth. When we drove up on the church ground, I could feel the anointing. The atmosphere was very welcoming. I felt like God had welcomed me home. God is welcoming, (Psalms 145:18) "The Lord is near to all who call on him, to all who call on him in truth." Finally, I decided I would join St. James Church. Once I joined St. James, my thirst for the Word was finally being quenched. I began growing spiritually, and Bishop Holder was teaching me so much. Within a year of being there, Raymond and I got married.

When God cleaned me up, he truly made me whole. I began my journey to Walking Worthy. Leviticus 20:8 states, "And ye shall keep my statutes, and do them. I am the Lord which sanctify you." I began working faithfully in the church. We had a small but faithful congregation. I was the Sunday school teacher, youth choir director, Sunday school secretary and worship leader. Our church was very active with the local churches, so we were always going, going and going. God began to speak to me, "It's time to answer my true calling." I ignored him. I wanted to make sure that God was calling me to ministry. I began to wonder, "What if this and what if that..." trying to make excuses. One of my what ifs was, "What if I lead someone astray?" Jeremiah 23:25 warns, "Woe be unto the pastors that destroy and scatter the sheep of my pasture saith the LORD." I didn't want that blood applied to my hands. I didn't ever want to be accountable because I caused someone to turn back to sin. I wanted to be walking worthy of my calling. Luke 12:48 also states, "For unto whomever much is given, of him shall be much required."

I would never say anything to Bishop Holder about anything God was saying. I wouldn't discuss my fears and the fact that I was not ready. However, God began to send opportunities for me to do sermonettes. Through my years at St. James, Bishop Holder instilled in the members to always remember our first love, God. He explained that it's important to be just as excited to run this Christian journey as the first day we got saved. He taught the members to always repent and do our first works over. Revelation 2:4-5 tells us, "Nevertheless, I have this against you, that you have left your first love. Remember therefore from where

11

you have fallen; repent and do the first works, or else I will come to you quickly and remove your lampstand from its place—unless you repent."

God has been water to quench my thirst (John 4:13-14). The more I served God the more I grew spiritually. The more I grew spiritually, the more I would hear the voice of God. I still wasn't ready for anything other than what I was comfortable doing, just being a servant. When I got invitations to do sermonettes, I was humbled by the opportunity to serve God. I prayed and asked God for the words to say and what to speak on. God began to say, "Study the word, and when you open your mouth, I'll speak through you." Anytime I speak a Word to God's people, I allow God to do the talking. 2 Samuel 23:2 reads, "The Spirit of the LORD speaks by me; his word is on my tongue."

I accepted to speak on two occasions. I spoke on the parable of the Sower (Matt 13:1-23). Then I received an invitation to speak on a woman of the Bible program at St. Matthews in Zebulon NC. I spoke on the book of Ruth. The closer I got to God, the more I began to hear God calling me to serve more. I began to run from the works God had for me. I would find excuses and reasons not to serve God anymore. Finally, I left the church to keep from moving forth in the work God had for me. Bishop Holder never truly knew why I was running, but I kept running from the Lord. I was afraid, and I felt I was not ready for that type of service. God is omniscient. I knew that God knew my heart. "The Lord searcheth all hearts, and understandeth all (1 Chr. 28:9)."

Through the years, I would visit other churches. Longing to be in fellowship and having a thirst for the Word, I finally joined another church. Proverbs 27:17 reveals, "Iron sharpeneth iron; so a man sharpeneth the countenance of his friend." I joined the adult choir and became an usher for a while. I learned really quick that ushering just was not for me, so I stopped. I enjoyed the Word. The pastor was awesome, a true man of God. Although the leaders and members of that church appreciated me and made me welcome, I was missing something. I didn't feel whole like I did at St. James. Spiritually, I felt a void. Something was missing. I learned a lot while I was there though. In mid-2010, I finally left. Again, I started visiting other churches. The services were awesome, and God was truly moving in the place.

Chapter Three

It's Time to Stop Running

I WAS TIRED OF running from God. I was tired of not having a church home. I wanted more than just a church to visit. God began to stir my spirit. God was saying, "It's time to be in a home church where my husband would join." Although I was welcome where I visited, and there was work to do, it wasn't my home. I began to pray for direction. I needed God to show me my home church. I was ready to be a faithful worker in the church. About a month later, I was invited to visit Delightful Temple Ministries one Sunday. I went and I was truly moved by the presence of the Lord. I felt a welcoming spirit like I felt when I would arrive at St. James. Yet again it was as if God had welcomed me home. God began to let me know he had answered my prayers and guided me to a church home. God is an advisor. Proverbs 19:20 says, "Listen to advice and accept instruction, that you may gain wisdom in the future."

All I know is I was tired of running from God. God blessed me with a great church home and an awesome church family. I'm grateful to have a church home that Raymond was happy to join. God blessed me with a church that had work for me. The pastor took me in and offered me the opportunity to serve. He also made sure I was no longer able to run from what God had for me. I no longer had any excuses. I began to walk in my calling as a minister. 2 Timothy 1:9 reveals, "Who hath saved us, and called us with a holy calling, not according to our works, but according to his own purpose and grace, which was given us."

Like the old saints used to say, "I believe I'll run on and see what the end is gonna be." All I can say is God is all-knowing. Psalm 37:4-5 states, "Delight yourself in the Lord, and he will give you the desires of your heart. Commit your way to the Lord; trust in him, and he will act." God is my Everything. He has been better to me than I have been to myself. On this Christian journey, I have grown spiritually and truly learned to walk worthy of calling myself a child of God.

CHAPTER FOUR

It's Cleansing Time

"Create in me a clean heart, O God; and renew a right spirit within me." *Psalm 51:10*

WHEN I GAVE MY life to Christ, I had to make a change. In order to walk worthy as a child of God, I knew I needed to be spiritually cleansed. It wasn't enough to just get saved. I needed to be converted. What does it mean to be converted? I'm glad you asked. To be converted means: God is now getting the sin and unrighteousness out of me. When I got saved, I was rescued from sin. I was freed from the arms of Satan and placed in the arms of God. Colossians 1:13-14 tells us, "For he has rescued us from the dominion of darkness and brought us into the kingdom of the Son he loves, in whom we have redemption, the forgiveness of sins." To be converted means, to come again. God is always trying to get us back to our original state that Adam was in before he sinned. Conversion is when we truly begin to change from the old man to the new. I needed to get rid of a lot of excess baggage, the things that weighed me down and held me back. Sometimes

17

we get so comfortable on this Christian journey that we forget to check our inventory and we become spiritual hoarders. Ephesians 4:22-24 reminds us, "That ye put off concerning the former conversation the old man, which is corrupt according to the deceitful lusts; and be renewed in the spirit of your mind, And that ye put on the new man, which after God is created in righteousness and true holiness." Until I was converted, my growth was stunted. As a child of God, I knew I should be growing spiritually just as I grow naturally. In the natural, I came into the world as a baby but through the years, I learned and grew. I started out on milk and gradually started eating meat. In the same way, I should be learning and growing spiritually. It does not matter how long I've been in church. It doesn't matter if my parents and grandparents went to church. It doesn't matter if I have titles and positions. I can't cleanse myself. Instead, I must draw near to God for myself and ask Him to do the cleansing. This is where transformation takes place. Transform means to develop the mind and character of Christ. Romans 12:2 instructs us, "And be not conformed to this world: but be ye transformed by the renewing of your mind, that ye may prove what is that good, and acceptable, and perfect, will of God."

I must be able to think and act like Christ to be effective in life and in ministry. Transformation is an actual saving and delivering process of the mind. Matthew 5:1-10 tells us, Jesus taught transformation of the mind. In order to grow spiritually and walk worthy, I had to cleanse myself of anything that was not of God. The characters of Jesus are the fruits of the spirit. Galatians 5:22 says, "But the fruit of the Spirit is love, joy, peace, longsuffering, gentleness, goodness, faith, meekness, temperance: against such there is no law." Transformation is an actual saving and delivering process of the mind. In the beatitudes, Jesus taught transformation of the mind. My duty as a Christian is to get God's Word in my heart. Psalm 119: 11 states, "Thy word have I hid in mine heart. That I might not sin against thee." Spiritual cleansing requires deep cleaning--it goes beyond what others see and hear. It's a cleansing from within, inside and out. As my heart gets clean, my language should follow. My conversations should be different. This is not just talking about bad language, cussing and vulgar language. It is also the lying, gossiping, repeating everything I hear and toting news. Luke 6:45 tells us, "A good man out of the good treasure of his heart bringeth forth that which is good; and an evil man out of the evil treasure of his heart bringeth forth that which is evil: for of the abundance of the heart his mouth speaketh." In other words, if my heart has been filled by the Spirit of God, my mouth will begin to speak like God does. I had to learn to let my yeas be yeas and my nays be nays. I learned to speak life on those dead situations. I learned to pray about things instead of fussing and always responding with a negative reaction. My mouth is a tool which can be used for good or bad. With my mouth, I can pray for myself and others. With my mouth, I can bless someone, and with the same mouth, I can curse someone. Amen!!! Proverbs 18:21 says, "Death and life are in the power of the tongue." The tongue can be used as a weapon to harm and destroy or as a tool to build and heal. I have to stop and ask myself, "What kind of impact do your words have? Are you walking worthy as a child of God?" This includes the challenge to stop complaining. When I find myself about to say something I don't need to be saying, I start praying. Father, God help me!! Or I start quoting scripture. Psalm 34 states, "I will bless the Lord at all times: his praise shall continually be in my mouth." Or start praising the Lord THANK YOU JESUS!! To God Be the Glory!! Or start humming um-mmmm, singing or something that's pleasing to God. Often times, we block our own blessings by talking too much. In order to walk worthy as a Christian, I had to renew my mind. Our mind needs renewal from the strongholds of the old ways of thinking and reasoning. What is a stronghold? The Webster's definition states, a place where a particular cause or belief is strongly defended or upheld. Our mind is a playground for the enemy. We have mental strongholds: spirits of confusion, generational curses, unbelief, spirits of misunderstanding etc. Renewing our mind requires faith, and faith is acting on the Word of God. My way of thinking should be different. I should be able to see things in the spiritual realm and not always in the natural. The renewing of the mind brings my will into agreement with my Father's will. As I fill your mind with His Word by reading, thinking about, memorizing, praying, speaking out loud, even singing, I begin to think in a way that pleases Him, and His ways become my ways. I become, through His power and wisdom, a master of my circumstances. 2 Cor 10:5 says, "Casting down imaginations, and every high thing that exalteth itself against the knowledge of God and bringing into captivity every thought to the obedience of Christ;" God is able to renew our mind if we let him; this is free will. However, we must surrender all to Him. God has a plan for our lives and surrendering to Him means we set aside our own plans and eagerly seek His. I had to learn to put God first in ALL things. Matthew 6: 33, 34 instructs, "But seek ye first the kingdom of God, and his righteousness; and all these things shall be added unto you. Take therefore no thought for the morrow."

Isaiah 10:27 tells us that it is the anointing that destroys the yokes of bondage in our lives! Yokes are like burdens we carry around. They are bondages that need to be broken off in order for us to be free. The anointing is God's presence in our lives helping us to do what He calls and leads us to do. Jesus is the Anointed One. He is the anointing that abides in me. His Spirit in me ministers that anointing to me regularly when I know how to receive it.

Since I have been given a free will, my mind needs

to discern between the old man and the new. This cannot take place unless the strongholds that satan built in my mind are broken. Only then can my mind become renewed and useful for God to reign. In order to walk a godly walk, I must surrender myself to God and be free from all those strongholds.

"Wherefore seeing we also are compassed about with so great a cloud of witnesses, let us lay aside every weight, and the sin which doth so easily beset us, and let us run with patience the race that is set before us." *Hebrews 12:1*

CHAPTER FIVE

I am a Living Testimony

"And the peace of God, which passeth all understanding, shall keep your hearts and minds through Christ Jesus." *Philippians 4:7*

WHEN I THINK OF the goodness of Jesus and all He has done for me, my soul cries out Hallelujah. I thank God for saving me. Thank God for second chances. I thank Him for the many times He has spared my life from seen and unseen dangers. I've seen many near death experiences during my lifetime. None of them can compare to the one on September 14, 2014 at approximately 2:38 AM. I almost died. I was down for the count, but God said not so. On Saturday evening of September 13, 2014, I went to bed feeling healthy like any other night. I wasn't feeling sick, and I hadn't done anything out of the norm. Later that night, I awoke from a deep sleep to use the restroom. While in the restroom, I began to feel sick. I felt nauseated, then I felt like I was about to pass out. I was thinking, Lord, what in the world? There were all types of thoughts racing through my head. On this particular night, my husband

Raymond never heard me get up. I was thinking, *if I pass out in the restroom, he won't know it.* I knew I would have help if I could at least make it back to the bed. I managed to make it to the bed but wasn't able to get on the bed. Our bed sits high, and I didn't have the strength to climb. I wasn't able to call out to Raymond. All I was able to do was lie down on the floor alongside the bed to keep from falling down. In the midst of trying to lie down to keep from falling, I felt the strange need to know the time.

The digital clock on my nightstand read 2:38 AM. As I lay there on the floor, I began to get cold. I felt my body began to shut down. It felt like there was a decrease in my blood circulation. Then, it seemed like my vital organs were stopping. During this time, I heard my husband say, "Di what are you doing on the floor?" I wasn't able to move and couldn't respond. Meanwhile, I was still lying there helpless. While lying there, I knew I was actually dying. Next, I felt when my bowel muscles relaxed. I felt the coldness flow down my legs and to my feet. It felt like someone had poured ice water in my bloodstream. Then, in an instant, I could feel my body functioning as normal. I felt my blood circulating like normal again. My body warmed up, and I was able to move and speak. Hallelujah! To God be all the glory! I began to pray and thank God for my life. I knew He had spared me for a reason. I slowly got up off the floor and got into bed. I didn't tell Raymond right then. I didn't want to frighten my husband and have him staring at me the rest of the night. Later, that morning I began to explain to him why I was on the floor. That afternoon I had called and explained everything to my daughter Renee. I told that Renee God knew I had some works that were left undone. I began to discuss some matters with Renee that needed to be handled in the event of untimely demise. Later that day, I was telling a friend about my experience. They laughed and asked, "Why did you need to know what time it was, had you died who were you gone tell?" I laughed and said, "I don't know, I just know at the time it was relevant."

Now, I know why the time was relevant. God knew what He was doing. He spared me and I'm able to tell my story. I was so close to death I began to wonder why, why do God spare my life? Maybe He did it to get my attention. All I know is I began to take inventory of my life. Was I headed to heaven or hell? Prior to that date, I thought nothing could separate me from the love of God. Romans 8:38,39 reads, "For I am persuaded, that neither death, nor life, nor angels, nor principalities, nor powers, nor things present, nor things to come, Nor height, nor depth, nor any other creature, shall be able to separate us from the love of God, which is in Christ Jesus our Lord." I was living righteous and serving God. I was studying the word. I was humble. I would pray and ask God to forgive my transgressions. I would even ask Him to forgive those that trespassed against me. Mark 11:25 instructs, "And whenever you stand praying, forgive, if you have anything against anyone, so that your Father also who is in heaven may forgive you your trespasses." As I began to examine myself, I began to ask, "Had I died, is there anything at all that would have separated me from God?" While processing these thoughts, I began to realize just how easy I had let my guard down. In 1 Peter 5:8-9, the scripture states, "We must be sober-minded and watchful. Satan is always on the prowl, waiting for an opportunity, for a crack to slip into."

To let down our guard against sin for even a moment gives him the moment he has been waiting for. His whole desire is to turn us from God. If we are watching and praying, then we can always resist him, firm in our faith, knowing that the same kinds of suffering are being experienced by our brotherhood throughout the world. While I was pondering on whether I was living my very best as a Christian, I thought of the seven churches in the book of Revelation. I thought about how the seven churches had fallen short. The Apostle John received a revelation from Jesus Christ, which is what we now call the book of Revelation. In this vision, Christ gave John seven messages for seven first-century churches in Asia Minor. Christ explained to each church what they'd done correctly and their shortcomings. I begin to reflect on so many things. While I was searching my heart, I asked myself, "What are your shortcomings? Have you truly forgiven people. Had I died that night what would God have told me about Diane? Have I forgiven family, friends, ex coworkers even my enemies? Have I forgiven the loved one that attacked my character? Have I forgiven the person that lied on me? Have I forgiven my debtors. What about the people that deliberately never paid what they owed me? What about the people that always made excuses to keep from paying their bail debts? Yet, I allowed them to be free because of the God in me. Many times, I would go out of my way to help someone because they asked. Yet they would always bite the hand that fed them. Had I forgiven those people? Was there any malice that I was harboring in my heart for those people? (John 10:10) The thief comes only to steal and kill and destroy. I came that they may have life and have it abundantly. This scripture is not talking about nor limited to material things. The enemy will steal your joy, kill your peace, and destroy your relationship with God if you're not watchful. Galatians 5:22-23 tells us, "But the fruit of the Spirit is love, joy, peace, patience, kindness, goodness, faithfulness, gentleness, self-control; against such things there is no law."

On that day, I realized I do not love anyone that much that I'm going to hell because of who they are. I began to pray like Jesus in Luke 23:34, "Father, forgive them for they know not what they do." I began to pray for them like I've never prayed before. I began to forgive the unpaid debts and cleaned the slate with a zero balance. God gave me peace with those that had taken advantage of my kindness. I bounced back and realized that every day is new opportunity for a closer walk with God. I learned that what I thought was my best wasn't good enough. I've faithfully worked on letting stuff go no matter how much it hurts. When I forgive, I have peace that only God can give. Philippians 4:7 states, "And the peace of God, which surpasses all understanding, will guard your hearts and minds through Christ Jesus." Now, I'm very careful not to allow the snares of the enemy to separate me from the love of God. God is my protector. No weapon that is formed against me shall prosper. He reminded me of 1 Chronicles 16:21,22, "He suffered no man to do them wrong: yea, he reproved kings for their sakes, Saying, touch not mine anointed, and do my prophets no harm." I have truly included forgiveness for others in my everyday walk. With that forgiveness, I continue to have my peace.

....

CHAPTER SIX

Blessed Quietness

"For we wrestle not against flesh and blood, but against principalities, against powers, against the rulers of the darkness of this world, against wickedness in high places."
Ephesians 6:12

BLESSED QUIETNESS! HOLY QUIETNESS! What assurance in my soul! I am a living testimony that God will give you perfect peace. God gives a peace that no man can understand. Philippians 4:7 says, "And the peace of God, which surpasses all understanding, will guard your hearts and minds through Christ Jesus. When we walk in spiritual authority, we can humble ourselves. The unction of the Holy Spirit will let us know when to speak and when to be silent. There have been many times along this Christian journey that I could have spoken with bitterness. I could have cussed someone out or even ripped their emotions to shreds with my mouth. There were times I wanted to say some harsh words to some awful people. There were times my garments and outward appearance were frowned upon. I've experienced people that say they are sanctified Christians yet they're jealous of the anointing that's on my life. The same sanctified Christians get upset every time God opens a door for me. But the God in me always smiles and say, "Bless you my brother or bless you my sister." There were many times along this journey that I was down for the count. But glory to God I was able to bounce back from life's blows. Thank God for guarding my mouth and bridling my tongue. Psalm141:3 says, "Set a guard, O Lord, before my mouth; keep the door of my lips." I thank God for blessing me to know when to speak. God blessed me to keep my mouth closed and continue studying the word. God is not concerned with our outward appearance but the matters of the heart. 1 Peter 3:3-4 states, "Whose adorning let it not be that outward adorning of plaiting the hair, and of wearing of gold, or of putting on of apparel; But let it be the hidden man of the heart, in that which is not corruptible, even the ornament of a meek and quiet spirit."

God does not look at the outward appearance. The hair, the jewelry, and the clothes mean nothing. God looks at the inner man. God is searching for a meek and quiet spirit. His word says, "A quiet spirit is more valuable to him." When someone is talking foolish or saying hurtful things just to get a response, I look at that devil with the authority which God have given me and say, "To God Be the Glory" or "Blessed Assurance Jesus Is Mine." I have to know who I am. I'm a child of the King! And I'm walking in spiritual authority. I shut up and allow God to do the speaking. I thank God for blessing me to know when to speak. Ecclesiastes 3:7 tells us "A <u>time</u> to <u>rend</u>, and a <u>time</u> to <u>sew</u>; a <u>time</u> to <u>keep silence</u>, and a <u>time</u> to <u>speak</u>."

When I get ready to speak on something that I know is not pleasing to God, I shut up and began to pray. Psalm 19:14 tells us, "Let the words of my mouth, and the meditation of my heart, be acceptable in thy sight, O LORD, my strength, and my redeemer." In other words, let my mouth speak nothing but what is true, kind, and profitable; and my heart meditate nothing but what is holy and pure. I choose to walk worthy of calling myself a Christian. The only way I can walk worthy is to surrender all of me to God. Surrendering all means I have to yield to the power of God. I have to love people regardless of how they carry themselves. I am a child of God and I have chosen to walk worthy.

After I launched my first book as a published author, Walking Worthy was birthed. Walking Worthy is my outreach ministry. The scripture God gave me for my outreach ministry is Colossians 1:10, "That ye may walk worthy of the Lord unto all pleasing, being fruitful in every good work, and increasing in the knowledge of God." Some people chose not to support my book simply because they played no part in it. Those naysayers did not know that was a prophecy on May 28, 2017 during altar call, it was prophesied that I would write books. In early 2018, I met my publisher, Felicia Lucas, at a Polish Your Diamond seminar. Felicia explained to me that she was looking for authors to be a part of her anthology. At that moment, the prophecy never crossed my mind. In fact, it wasn't until after the book launched, and I began to see that the naysayers had chosen not to support the book. Some thought their dirty laundry was being aired and some just simply had their reasons. Keep in mind these were people that call themselves sanctified Christians.

My husband and I were so disappointed by the negative behavior of people that say they are "saved." Yet, we kept our mouths closed and took it to God in prayer. Proverbs 17:27-28 says, "He who has knowledge spares his words, and a man of understanding is of a calm spirit. Even a fool is counted wise when he holds his peace; when he shuts his lips, he is considered perceptive.

I had gotten to a point that I was asking God what makes mankind so jealous. When we say we are Christians, doesn't that mean to be Christ-like? Where is it written that Christ was like this? Why can't those of us that claim to be Christians be happy and supportive of others? I could remember being in the presence of some Christians, and I felt like Superman around kryptonite. God reminded me that everyone that is saved is not delivered. Ephesians 6:12 reminds us, "For we wrestle not against flesh and blood, but against principalities, against powers, against the rulers of the darkness of this world, against wickedness in high places." Also, Isaiah 58:3 lets us know that sin separates us from God. My mind went back to when I first answered my calling into ministry. I was told that everyone can't go where I'm going. I must say, after Down for The Count launched, and I had to deal with some serious demons. Again, these were people that call themselves sanctified Christians. I remember spending so much time praying, seeking Godly wisdom.

Two weeks later, God began to let me know these are doors that He had opened for me. As I was praying one day, God spoke to my spirit and said, "This is the prophecy that Prophetess Julia Walker had spoken to you last year," "It was my promise that you would write books." God let me know I didn't need to apologize to anyone for being blessed. I didn't need to apologize because I'm anointed. I didn't need to apologize because he was exalting me. Glory to God! I was able to bounce back from life's blows. God is my keeper. Psalm 121:5 says, "The Lord is thy keeper: the Lord is thy shade upon thy right hand." God guards my mouth. Also Proverbs 21:23 states, "Whoso keepeth his mouth and his tongue keepeth his soul from troubles. Isaiah 30:15 goes on to say, "For thus saith the Lord GOD, the Holy One of Israel; In returning and rest shall ye be saved; in quietness and in confidence shall be your strength: and ye would not." We must be born again. When we are born again Christians turning to God, He will give us rest. I had to trust in God, full of calmness and of peace. All praise belongs to God. None of the foolishness made me bitter; it made me better. It didn't break me. It made me stronger. By the grace of God, I remained steadfast and immovable always abounding in the works of the Lord. I know that my labor in the Lord is not in vain. Amen. Romans 15:13 tells us, "May the God of hope fill you with all joy and peace as you trust in him, so that you may overflow with hope by the power of the Holy Spirit."

My Prayer

OUR FATHER, WHICH ART in Heaven. Forgive us for our sins, known and unknown. Father God, I pray that your Word blesses someone on today. I pray that someone will be healed from the inside out. Lord, bless that person with the unforgiving spirit to be able to cry out to you and release the unforgiveness. Heal the brokenness. Remove the hurt, Father God. Touch our hearts, our mouths and our minds, Lord Jesus. Lord, bless us to learn how to walk worthy of saying we are born again Christians. Teach us to glorify You, Lord Jesus. Bless each of us to walk in the light so that we may spend eternity with you. In Jesus' name, I pray. Amen.

ABOUT THE AUTHOR

DIANE PACE was born in Smithfield, NC and now resides in Wendell, NC. Diane is the daughter of the late Willie Harvey Turner II and Frances Turner. Through that union she is the youngest of seven siblings. She is a loving wife to her husband Raymond Pace. She is a mother of six children. She has nine grandchildren and one great grandchild. She is the Founder of Walking Worthy. She is a Co Author in Down for The Count; Bouncing Back from Life's Blows Volume I and II. She is the Membership Coordinator and Public Relations Assistant for Women of Triumph Ministries. Diane is also a Mentor for the Daughter and Sisters of Triumph Ministry. She is a Minister at Delightful Temple Ministries in Kenly, NC under the leadership of Pastor Carolynn Robinson and Deacon Moses Robinson.

Email: walkingworthyisa@yahoo.com

MY WALKING WORTHY JOURNAL

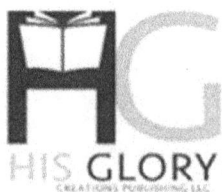

His Glory Creations Publishing, LLC is an International Christian Book Publishing Company, which provides publishing services for clients. They help launch and scale the creative works of new, aspiring and seasoned authors across the globe, through stories that are inspirational, empowering, life-changing or educational in nature, including fiction and non-fiction.

Contact Information:
CEO/Founder: Felicia C. Lucas
Website: www.hisglorycreationspublishing.com
Email: hgcpublishingllc@gmail.com
Phone: 919-679-1706

www.ingramcontent.com/pod-product-compliance
Lightning Source LLC
LaVergne TN
LVHW041208080426
835508LV00008B/860